# HISTORIC PHOTOS OF
# THOMAS EDISON

## TEXT AND CAPTIONS BY LEONARD DEGRAAF

TURNER
PUBLISHING COMPANY
NASHVILLE, TENNESSEE    PADUCAH, KENTUCKY

Edison with his miner's safety lamp in 1923. Edison failed to create a market for battery-powered automobiles, but he adapted his storage battery for other industrial applications, designing a lightweight battery to power miners' lamps. These batteries did not release dangerous gases that could cause explosions in underground mines. His storage batteries were also used to power lighthouses, railroad signals, and small boats.

# HISTORIC PHOTOS OF
# THOMAS EDISON

Turner Publishing Company
200 4th Avenue North • Suite 950     412 Broadway • P.O. Box 3101
Nashville, Tennessee 37219      Paducah, Kentucky 42002-3101
(615) 255-2665          (270) 443-0121

www.turnerpublishing.com

*Historic Photos of Thomas Edison*

Library of Congress Control Number: 2007929647

ISBN-13: 978-1-59652-406-4

Printed in the United States of America

08 09 10 11 12 13 14 15—0 9 8 7 6 5 4 3 2 1

# CONTENTS

Edison outside the office of his Ogdensburg, New Jersey, ore milling plant in 1895. During the 1890s, Edison developed technology to process low-grade iron ore. In 1889, he created the New Jersey & Pennsylvania Concentrating Works, which financed an experimental ore milling plant in northeastern New Jersey.

# Acknowledgments

This volume, *Historic Photos of Thomas Edison,* is the result of the cooperation and efforts of many individuals and organizations. It is with great thanks that we acknowledge the valuable contribution of the Edison National Historic Site for their generous support.

Thanks also to former acting superintendent Randy W. Turner for approving this project, the Friends of Edison National Historic Site for their support, and Edward Wirth, Michelle Ortwein, Greg Schmidl, and the staff of Edison National Historic Site for their assistance.

# PREFACE

The images in this book, selected from the Edison National Historic Site historic photograph collection, illustrate Thomas A. Edison's long career as an inventor, entrepreneur, and public figure. They also reveal his private life, including Edison relaxing at home with his children, vacationing with his family in Florida, and traveling with his closest friends.

Edison rose from modest circumstances to become one of the most prolific and influential inventors in United States history, ultimately securing 1,093 U.S. patents, the record for the highest number of patents granted to an individual. He is perhaps best known as the inventor of the phonograph, the first practical incandescent electric lamp, and the motion picture camera—inventions that formed the basis of the electric light and electric power, sound recording, and motion picture industries.

Edison also made significant improvements to the telegraph and telephone, devised new methods to process iron ore and manufacture Portland cement, invented storage batteries for electric vehicles and other purposes, designed a process for constructing cement houses, and searched for new sources of domestic rubber. During World War I, Edison conducted research for the U.S. Navy aimed at protecting commercial shipping from enemy submarines. He also invented the electric pen, a forerunner of the mimeograph, and the fluoroscope, an early X-ray instrument.

Edison pioneered team-based industrial research at his Menlo Park and West Orange, New Jersey, laboratories. These laboratories fostered technical creativity and innovation by bringing together the skilled experimenters, tools, supplies, and other resources Edison needed to produce new inventions on a regular basis. The Menlo Park and West Orange laboratories served as models for the research and development facilities created by governments, corporations, and universities in the early twentieth century.

Edison was also an entrepreneur and business leader. From the early 1870s to the late 1920s, he created and managed dozens of companies to manufacture and market his inventions. For Edison, technical innovation involved more than solving technical problems in his laboratories. He also raised capital to finance his companies, established manufacturing facilities, identified potential markets for his inventions, and tailored marketing and advertising strategies to reach those markets.

Edison was one of the most recognized public figures of the late nineteenth and early twentieth centuries. A test of this notoriety came in April 1911, when a drugstore in Wilson, North Carolina, mailed Edison a letter with only his photograph on the envelope. Inside the envelope, a letter explained to Edison that during "an argument in our store a few days since about the best known picture in the U.S. your name was mentioned and we said that your picture was known well enough to carry a letter to you without any address on [the] envelope." The letter reached Edison's desk in thirteen days.

Contemporaries recognized Edison because he used his image to promote his inventions. Edison's face and signature appeared in his advertising material and product packaging. Edison employed photographers at his Menlo Park and West Orange laboratories to document his work or create photographs for legal, administrative, or advertising purposes. Some of these images capture candid moments, but many others were carefully staged portraits of Edison working in his laboratories or posing with his inventions.

Many of Edison's photographs were produced for consumption by the public. The West Orange laboratory's photography department provided a steady stream of prints to fulfill photograph requests from Edison's admirers. Press photographers created images of Edison to illustrate newspaper and magazine articles. Other photographs, including candid shots and studio portraits of Edison and his family, preserved private memories. For whatever reason they were created, the approximately 60,000 historic photographs in the Edison National Historic Site archives provide a nearly complete photographic record of Edison's professional and personal life.

Thomas Alva Edison was born in this brick house in Milan, Ohio, on February 11, 1847. Nicknamed "Al," he was the youngest of seven children born to Samuel and Nancy Elliott Edison.

# THE EARLY YEARS

## (1847–1875)

Thomas Edison was born on February 11, 1847, in Milan, Ohio. In 1854 his family moved to Port Huron, Michigan. By most accounts, Edison had a typical childhood, but traits that later helped him succeed as an inventor, including an intense curiosity and capacity for hard work, emerged early in his life. As a boy Edison was particularly interested in science and technology. He read books on physics and chemistry and tinkered with machines. Archeological evidence uncovered at the site of his Port Huron home reveals that he had a chemistry set, complete with chemicals, glass beakers, and test tubes.

The railroads and telegraph lines spreading across the United States in the 1850s gave Edison his first professional experiences. From 1859 to 1863, he was a newspaper vendor on the Grand Trunk Railroad between Port Huron and Detroit. In 1863 he learned Morse code, allowing him to join the growing ranks of skilled telegraph operators during the Civil War. Between 1863 and 1868, Edison worked as an itinerant telegrapher throughout the Midwest and South, devoting his spare time to reading and experimenting with telegraph equipment.

Edison became a telegrapher for Western Union in Boston in the spring of 1868. Boston was a center of technical innovation, providing aspiring inventors like Edison with access to machine shops, a community of experienced electricians, and investors eager to develop new inventions. In Boston, Edison signed his first patent applications for an electric vote recorder and a printing telegraph, an instrument that transmitted stock prices and other financial information. In January 1869, he announced his decision to become a full-time inventor.

Edison moved to New York City in the spring of 1869. In August he became superintendent of the Gold and Stock Telegraph Company and, later that year, established an electrical consulting business. Edison came to New York in part to be closer to the managers of the leading telegraph companies, who required faster, more reliable technology to meet the growing demand for their services and who could provide Edison with the financial and marketing support he needed to develop his inventions. By the winter of 1870, Edison had opened his first shop in Newark, New Jersey, where he designed and manufactured a variety of inventions for the telegraph industry.

Thomas's father, Samuel, was born in Nova Scotia in 1804, the son of British Loyalists who moved to Canada after the American Revolution. In 1811 his family settled in Vienna, Ontario. Samuel became an innkeeper and, in 1828, married Nancy Elliott. He fled to the United States in 1837 after provincial authorities indicted him for participating in a failed political rebellion. In 1839 Samuel moved his family to Milan, Ohio, a booming canal town near Lake Huron.

Edison's mother, Nancy, was born in Chenango County, New York, in 1810, the daughter of a Baptist minister who moved his family to Vienna, Ontario. Nancy taught school in Canada, experience that later helped her teach Thomas to read and write.

Thomas with his sister Harriet Ann (Tannie), around 1854. Three of Edison's six siblings died before his first birthday. An economic depression in Milan forced the Edison family to move to Port Huron, Michigan, in the spring of 1854. In Port Huron, Samuel worked as a vegetable farmer, lumber trader, and land speculator. Samuel also built and operated a local tourist attraction, an observation tower overlooking Lake Huron.

Thomas, shown here at age 14, received little formal instruction. He attended school briefly in Port Huron, but his mother provided most of his education at home. Edison later claimed that his teachers kicked him out of school because they thought he was "addled," but his family's lack of resources may have prevented longer school attendance.

Between 1859 and 1862, Edison worked as a newspaper and candy vendor on the Grand Trunk Railroad between Port Huron and Detroit. This photograph shows the interior of a replica baggage car built by Henry Ford for the 1929 Light's Golden Jubilee celebration. Edison recalled that the car "was supposed to be the smoking car but I never knew anybody to use it. It had no ventilation and cinders came through the cracks."

Edison stored his stock of newspapers and candy, a small collection of chemicals for experiments, and the printing press he used to publish the *Weekly Herald,* in the baggage end of the car. The railroad fired Edison after he tipped over a bottle of phosphorus and set the car on fire.

The February 3, 1862, issue of the *Weekly Herald,* the newspaper Edison published while working on the Grand Trunk Railroad. Printed with a second-hand press, the paper offered local news and gossip, farm prices, advertisements, and railroad schedules. Edison charged eight cents for a monthly subscription.

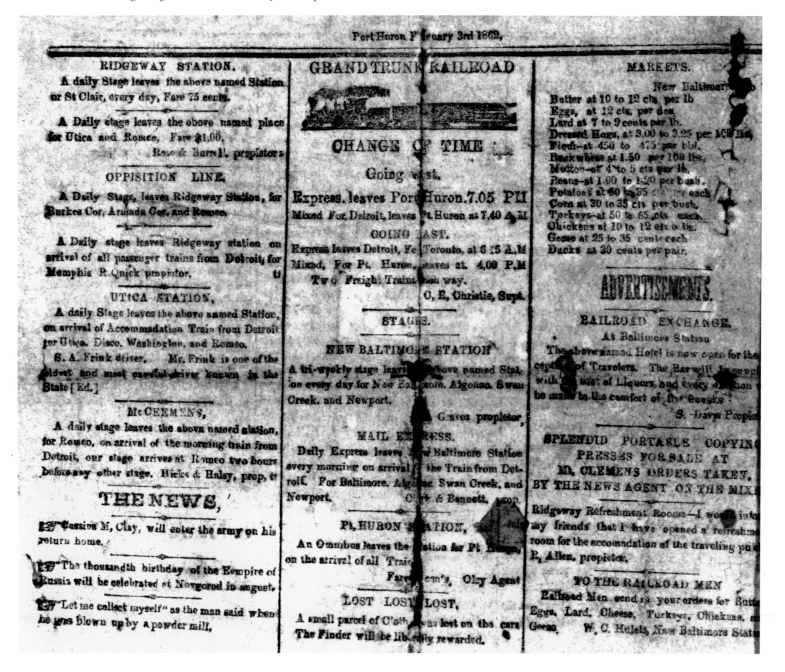

Port Huron February 3rd 1862.

### RIDGEWAY STATION.

A daily Stage leaves the above named Station or St Clair, every day, Fare 75 cents.

A Daily stage leaves the above named place for Utica and Romeo, Fare $1,00.

Rose & Burrell. propietors

### OPPISITION LINE.

A Daily Stage, leaves Ridgeway Station, for Burkes Cor, Armada Cor, and Romeo.

A Daily stage leaves Ridgeway station on arrival of all passenger trains from Detroit, for Memphis R. Quick propietor,

### UTICA STATION.

A daily Stage leaves the above named Station, on arrival of Accommadation Train from Detroit for Utica, Disco, Washington, and Romeo. S. A. Frink driver, Mr. Frink is one of the oldest and most carefull driver known in the State [ Ed.]

### McCEEMENS,

A daily stage leaves the above named station, for Romeo, on arrival of the morning train from Detroit, our stage arrives at Romeo two hours before any other stage. Hicks & Halsy, prop.

# THE NEWS,

Cassius M, Clay, will enter the army on his return home.

The thousandth birthday of the Eempire of Russia will be celebrated at Novgorod in august.

"Let me collect myself" as the man said when he was blown up by a powder mill.

### GRAND TRUNK RAILROAD

## CHANGE OF TIME

Going west.

Express. leaves Port Huron. 7.05 PM
Mixed For Detroit, leaves Pt. Huron at 7.40 A.M

GOING EAST.

Express leaves Detroit, For Toronto, at 6 15 A.M
Mixed, For Pt. Huron, leaves at 4.09 P.M
Two Freight Trains eas way.

C. E. Christie, Supt.

### STAGES.

### NEW BALTIMORE STATION

A tri-weekly stage leaves the above named Station every day for New Baltimore, Algonac, Swan Creek, and Newport.

Graves propietor,

### MAIL EXPRESS.

Daily Express leaves New Baltimore Station every morning on arrival of the Train from Detroit. For Baltimore, Algonac Swan Creek, and Newport. Clark & Bennett, prop.

### Pt. HURON STATION,

An Omnibus leaves the Station for Pt. Huron, on the arrival of all Trains

Fare cents, Oley Agent

### LOST LOST LOST.

A small parcel of Cloth was lost on the cars The Finder will be liberally rewarded.

### MARKETS.

New Baltimore
Butter at 10 to 12 cts per lb
Eggs, at 12 cts, per doz
Lard at 7 to 9 cents per lb.
Dressed Hogs, at 3.00 to 3.25 per 100 lbs,
Flesh—at 450 to 475 per bbl.
Buckwheat at 1.50 per 100 lbs,
Mutton—at 4 to 5 cts per lb.
Beans—at 1.00 to 1.20 per bush.
Potatoes at 30 to 35 cts per each
Corn at 30 to 35 cts per bush.
Turkeys—at 50 to 65 cts each
Chickens at 10 to 12 cts a lb.
Geese at 25 to 35 cents each
Ducks at 30 cents per pair.

## ADVERTISEMENTS.

### RAILROAD EXCHANGE.

At Baltimore Station

The above named Hotel is now open for the reception of Travelers. The Bar will be supplied with best of Liquors, and every exertion will be made to the comfort of the Guests

S. Davis Propie

SPLENDID PORTABLE COPYING PRESSES FOR SALE AT Mt. CLEMENS ORDERS TAKEN, BY THE NEWS AGENT ON THE MIXED

Ridgeway Refreshment Rooms—I would into my friends that I have opened a refreshme room for the accommodation of the traveling pub P, Allen, propietor,

### TO THE RAILROAD MEN

Railroad Men send in your orders for Butte Eggs, Lard, Cheese, Turkeys, Chickens, a Geese. W. C. Hulets, New Baltimore Statio

This 1913 photograph shows the Mount Clemens, Michigan, railroad station, where Edison learned telegraphy in the summer of 1863. Stationmaster James MacKenzie taught Edison Morse code in appreciation for saving his young son from a runaway freight car. These lessons enabled Edison to become a telegraph operator in Port Huron.

Edison signed the application for his first U.S. patent, an electric vote recorder, on October 13, 1868. The instrument allowed legislatures to automatically record their votes on bills. Edison attempted to sell the vote recorder to the U.S. Congress, but lawmakers were not interested in a machine that interfered with logrolling (vote trading). As a result, Edison vowed not to pursue inventions that did not have commercial markets.

Edison's vote recorder patent included this drawing. Patents give inventors the exclusive right to manufacture and market their inventions for a limited period of time, in exchange for revealing details about the invention's design and operation. Edison secured 1,093 U.S. patents in his lifetime, the highest number granted to an individual.

**T. A. EDISON.**

Electric Vote-Recorder.

No. 90,646.

Patented June 1, 1869.

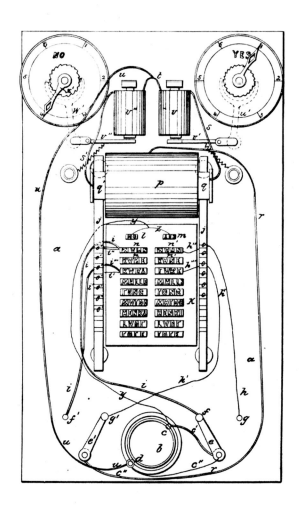

Inventor.
Thomas A Edison.

In January 1869, Edison announced his decision to become a professional inventor. That same month he signed a patent application for a new printing telegraph, which allowed banks and brokerage firms to quickly transmit stock prices to their customers. In 1870, Edison signed an agreement with the Gold and Stock Telegraph Company to continue developing printing telegraphs, an arrangement that enabled him to open his own manufacturing shop in Newark, New Jersey.

From 1870 to 1876, Edison operated two shops in Newark, the Newark Telegraph Works on Railroad Avenue and, after April 1871, this shop on Ward Street. During this period Edison designed and manufactured printing and automatic telegraphs. He also devised multiplex telegraph systems, which allowed the transmission of multiple messages over a single wire.

· A new system of Telegraphy, using neither dots nor dashes, but receiving the Message by a Puncher or Embosser and Running it through an automatic Translating Printing Machine I do not wish to confine myself to any particular Translating Printing Machine, as I have innumerable machines in my Mind now which I shall continue to Illustrate & describe day by day when I have the Spare time,

The Printer which I propose to use for translating from the punched or Embossed paper, is as follows though I May improve it in time or adopt an entirely new one using Magnetism or dispensing with it and make the paper perform a mechanical Operation,

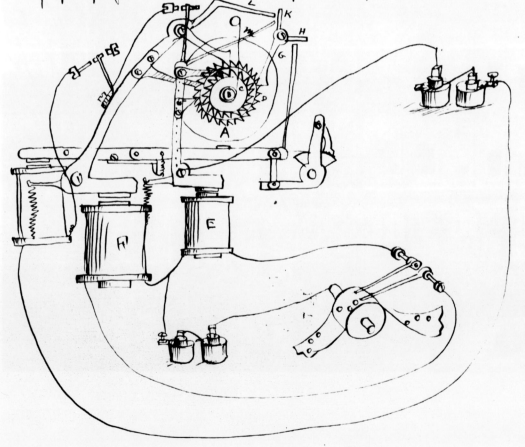

A is the type wheel B its shaft C is a small ratchet wheel rotated

Edison wrote this note on automatic telegraphy on August 5, 1871. The telegraph industry employed skilled operators to transmit and receive messages manually. To increase the speed and reliability of transmission, inventors like Edison devised systems able to send telegraph messages automatically on perforated strips of paper. At the receiving end, messages were recorded on chemically treated paper.

In 1875, Edison invented the electric pen, an instrument that produced document stencils. The electric pen consisted of a hand-held reciprocating needle that punched holes in sheets of wax paper. The operator then made copies by passing an ink roller over the stencil mounted in a special frame. A small electric motor, powered by a chemical battery, operated the pen from atop the needle.

# EDISON'S
# ELECTRIC PEN and PRESS
## ❦ 5000 ❦
## COPIES FROM A SINGLE WRITING.

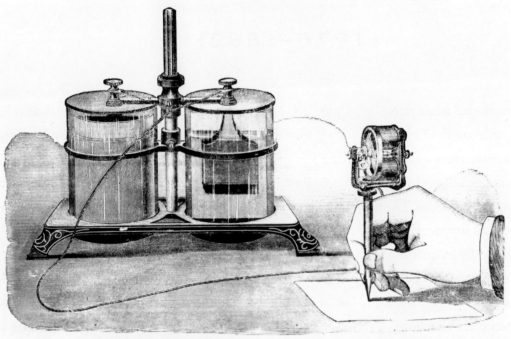

## THE ELECTRIC PEN AND DUPLICATING PRESS

Was invented three years ago.  Many thousands are now in use in the United States, Canada, Great Britain, France, Germany, Russia, Australia, New Zealand, Cuba, Brazil, China, Japan, and other countries.

Stencils can be made with the Electric Pen nearly as fast as writing can be done with an ordinary Pen.  From 1,000 to 15,000 impressions can be taken from each stencil, by means of the Duplicating Press, at the speed of five to fifteen per minute.

The apparatus is used by the United States, City and State Governments, Railroad, Steamboat and Express Companies, Insurance and other Corporations, Colleges and Schools, Churches, Sabbath Schools, Societies, Bankers, Real Estate Dealers, Lawyers, Architects, Engineers, Accountants, Printers, and Business Firms in every department of trade.

It is especially valuable for the cheap and rapid production of all matter requiring duplication, such as Circulars, Price Lists, Market Quotations, Business Cards, Autographic Circular Letters and Postal Cards, Pamphlets, Catalogues, Ruled and Blank Forms, Lawyers' Briefs, Contracts, Abstracts, Legal Documents, Freight Tariffs, Time Tables, Invoices, Labels, Letter, Bill and Envelope Heads, Maps, Tracings, Architectural and Mechanical Drawings, Plans and Specifications, Bills of Fare, Music, Insurance Policies, Cypher Books, Cable and Telegraphic Codes, Financial Exhibits, Property Lists, Manifests, Inventories, Schedules, Shipping Lists, College and School Documents, Rolls, Examination Questions, Examples, Illustrations, Scholars' Reports, Lecture Notes, Regulations, Blanks, Official Notices, Mailing Lists, Committee Reports, Sermons, Lectures, Pastoral Information, Manuscripts, Journals, Fac-Similies of Papers, Drawings, Hieroglyphics, Programmes, Designs, etc.

Circulars prepared with the Electric Pen pass through the mails as third class matter at one cent per ounce or fraction thereof.   Additional information and samples of work furnished on application.

PRICES—No. 1 Outfit, with 7×11 Press, $40.00.
" 2 " " 9×11 " 50.00.
" 3 " " 9×14 " 60.00.
Sent C.O.D., or on Receipt of Price.

### GEO. H. BLISS. GENERAL MANAGER, 220 TO 232 KINZIE STREET, CHICAGO.

| | |
|---|---|
| LOCAL AGENCY, 142 La Salle Street, Chicago. | PHILADELPHIA AGENCY, 628 Chestnut St., Philadelphia. |
| DOMINION AGENCY, 44 Church Street, Toronto, Ont. | GEN'L EASTERN AGENCY, 20 New Church St., New York. |

Advertisement for Edison's Electric Pen and Press, around 1878. Edison began marketing the electric pen in August 1875. Despite his belief that the pen would be widely used in offices, his sales agents had difficulty selling the instrument because of several technical defects. Edison's staff attempted to correct these defects as late as 1877. Eventually, Edison sold the electric pen to A. B. Dick, a Chicago manufacturer who introduced the mimeograph in 1884.

# Menlo Park Laboratory

## (1876–1882)

In March 1876, Edison opened a laboratory in Menlo Park, New Jersey, a small village on the Pennsylvania Railroad approximately twenty-five miles south of New York City. A legal dispute with a former landlord in Newark prompted Edison's move, but the money he received from a contract with the Western Union Telegraph Company to experiment on acoustic telegraphy enabled him to build the new laboratory. Menlo Park's rural setting provided seclusion and privacy, allowing Edison and his team to work without distractions. The laboratory's proximity to the railroad, however, gave Edison easy access to his corporate sponsors and financial supporters in New York.

Edison secured more than 400 patents at Menlo Park between 1876 and 1882. Initially he continued his telegraph research at the new laboratory but soon entered other fields. His work on the acoustic telegraph, which used sounds of different tones to transmit multiple messages over a single wire, led to his interest in the telephone. Western Union supported Edison's efforts to develop an alternative to Alexander Graham Bell's telephone, which was introduced in July 1876 at the Philadelphia Centennial Exhibition. The result was a carbon transmitter that improved the sound quality of Bell's telephone and an induction coil that boosted the distance a telephone signal could travel over electric wires.

Edison's acoustic telegraph and telephone research contributed to his discovery of the principle of sound recording in the summer of 1877. By the end of 1877, he had unveiled his tinfoil phonograph, the first machine to record and reproduce sound.

Edison began experimenting on electric lighting in the fall of 1878. The Menlo Park laboratory designed the first practical incandescent electric lamp, devised a system for producing and distributing electric power, and performed pioneering research on electric railroads. Edison also organized companies to generate and sell electric power, including the Edison Electric Illuminating Company of New York (which eventually became New York City's Con Edison) and a group of companies to manufacture electric lighting equipment that were later merged into General Electric.

By the early 1880s Edison's focus had shifted to the management of his electric lighting companies based in New York City. He closed the Menlo Park laboratory in November 1882.

In March 1876, Edison opened a laboratory in Menlo Park, New Jersey, a small village on the Pennsylvania Railroad several miles north of New Brunswick. At Menlo Park, Edison vowed to produce "a minor invention every ten days and a big thing every six months." From 1876 to 1882, Edison and his staff improved the telephone, invented the phonograph, and devised his incandescent electric lighting system.

Edison and his experimenters on the second floor of the Menlo Park laboratory in 1880. The laboratory's open floor plan encouraged communication between Edison and his workers. At Menlo Park, Edison created an informal environment designed to foster creativity and collaboration. There were no formal work rules, nor were experimenters governed by the time clock. Edison's team worked long hours, but they also enjoyed late-night meals, storytelling, and practical jokes.

Edison relied on skilled machinists, chemists, and draftsmen to develop his inventions. Between 1878 and 1882, he employed more than 200 experimenters. The number of workers rose or fell depending on Edison's needs. Some employees, seeking opportunities to learn about new electrical technologies, worked at Menlo Park briefly, while others remained with Edison for years and eventually assumed managerial positions in his manufacturing companies.

Charles Batchelor (1845–1910) was one of Edison's principal assistants in the 1870s and 1880s. Born in London and trained as a mechanic, Batchelor came to the United States in 1870 to install equipment at the Clark Sewing Thread Mill in Newark, New Jersey. He joined Edison at his Newark shop and played an important role in Edison's telephone, sound recording, and electric light research at Menlo Park.

John Kruesi (1843–1899) was a skilled Swiss-born machinist who joined Edison in 1871. Kruesi was adept at translating Edison's rough sketches into precise working prototypes.

Edison and his staff conducted extensive research on the telephone at Menlo Park in 1877 and 1878. They devised an improved transmitter, which increased the sound quality of Alexander Graham Bell's telephone. They also invented an induction coil, which allowed the telephone's signal to be transmitted over longer distances.

John Kruesi used this sketch in November 1877 to build Edison's tinfoil phonograph, the world's first sound recording instrument. The first words Edison recorded on the phonograph were a verse from the nursery rhyme "Mary Had a Little Lamb."

Edison unveiled the tinfoil phonograph on December 7, 1877, at the New York City office of *Scientific American,* the leading technical journal of the nineteenth century. The machine astonished the editor, who remarked "no matter how familiar a person may be with modern machinery . . . it is impossible to listen to the mechanical speech without his experiencing the idea that his senses are deceiving him."

In early 1878, Edison and his associates demonstrated the phonograph at Menlo Park and at public exhibitions throughout the Northeast. During an April 1878 visit to Washington, D.C., Edison demonstrated the phonograph at the Smithsonian Institution, at the U.S. Capitol for members of Congress, and at the White House for President Rutherford B. Hayes. During this trip, he posed for this photograph at Matthew Brady's studio.

After several months of promoting the phonograph and an even longer period working on the telephone, Edison appeared exhausted when he posed for this portrait in the spring of 1878. He continued working on these inventions until the summer, when he left Menlo Park for a month-long trip to the western United States.

In July 1878, Edison (second from right) traveled to Rawlins, Wyoming, with a group of astronomers to observe a solar eclipse. Edison joined the group to record the temperature of the sun's corona with his tasimeter, a sensitive heat-measuring instrument. After the expedition Edison visited San Francisco, Yosemite, Virginia City, Nevada, and the Colorado Rockies.

Edison invented the first practical incandescent lamp at Menlo Park. Incandescent lamps work by passing an electric current through a substance to the point where it "incandesces" or emits light. Other inventors had tried to devise an incandescent lamp as early as the 1840s, but before Edison began his electric light research in the fall of 1878 no one had found a material able to emit light for long periods of time before burning or melting.

Edison made this electric lamp sketch in a laboratory notebook on February 18, 1880. To prevent the lamp filament from burning, Edison enclosed the filament in a glass vacuum and designed a regulator to prevent the filament from heating to the melting point. Much of Edison's research focused on finding a suitable filament. Edison and his staff tested different materials, including platinum, nickel, celluloid, and coconut hair, before settling on carbonized bamboo.

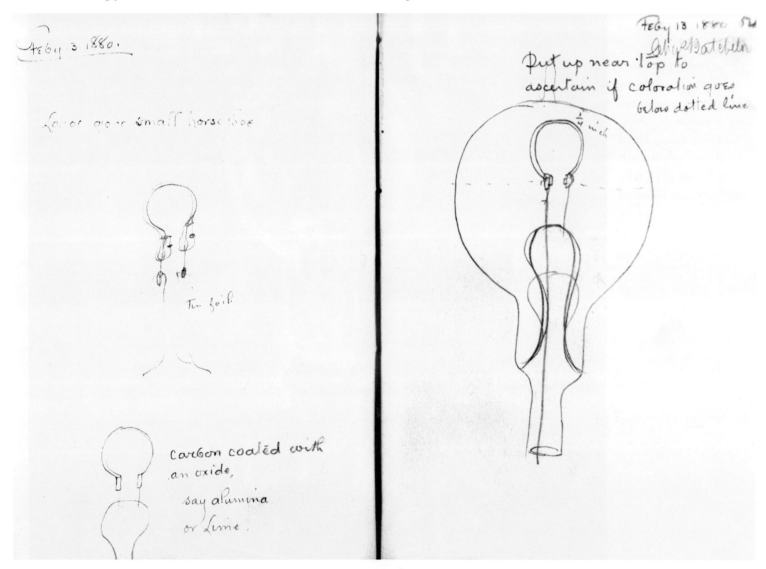

The development of an incandescent lamp required Edison and his staff to invent a system of components, including generators, switches, fuses, meters, and conductors. In March 1879, the Menlo Park Lab designed this generator, nicknamed the "long-legged Mary Ann" because of its distinctive iron poles.

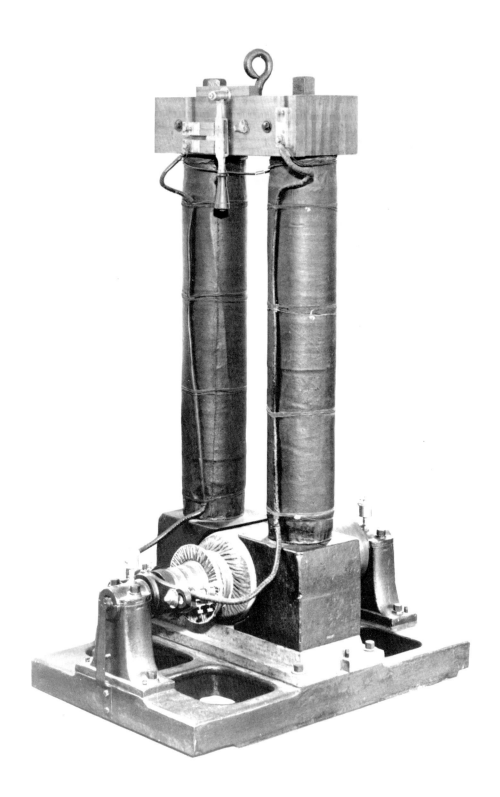

Employees of the Edison Lamp Works outside the Menlo Park factory in 1880. Edison created several companies to manufacture his electric lighting system, including the Edison Machine Works (dynamos) and the Electric Tube Company (underground conductors). In 1880, he established the Edison Lamp Company and began manufacturing lamps at his former electric pen factory in Menlo Park.

When Edison posed for this portrait in June 1881, the focus of his personal and professional life was shifting to New York City. In March of that year, he moved his residence to New York and opened an office at 65 Fifth Avenue to manage his electric light companies.

This drawing shows the dynamo room of Edison's Pearl Street central station. Opening on September 4, 1882, the Pearl Street station was the first commercial incandescent electric light utility in the United States. Initially, the station supplied power to 85 buildings wired for 2,323 lamps, located within a one-mile-square area of lower Manhattan. Its customers included Drexel, Morgan & Company, the New York Times, and the New York Stock Exchange.

To increase demand for the electric power supplied by his central stations, the Menlo Park laboratory devised an electric railroad motor. Edison's staff tested it on a track constructed in 1880 near the laboratory. Edison's daughter Marion later recalled, "I was always very happy when riding on his electric railway which was narrow gauge and led from the laboratory grounds to an abandoned copper mine."

As Edison constructed the West Orange laboratory in 1887, he claimed, "I will have the best equipped and largest laboratory extant, and the facilities incomparably superior to any other for the rapid & cheap development of an invention." The main laboratory building included a library, machine shops, experimental rooms, and a stock room. Separate buildings housed electrical, chemical, and metallurgical laboratories.

# West Orange Laboratory

## (1887–1931)

In 1887, Edison constructed a new laboratory in West Orange, New Jersey. Edison's move to West Orange was prompted by several changes in his personal and professional life during the 1880s. His first wife, Mary Stilwell Edison, died in August 1884. Edison married his second wife, Mina Miller, in February 1886. Shortly before their wedding, Edison purchased Glenmont, a thirteen-acre estate in Llewellyn Park, a private residential community in West Orange.

After he closed the Menlo Park laboratory in 1882, Edison spent most of his time working in the shops and offices of his electric lighting companies in New York City. Because he lacked sufficient space to continue his electric lighting research and develop other inventions, he purchased property less than a mile from Glenmont to build a new laboratory.

Edison opened the West Orange laboratory in early December 1887. The laboratory's three-story main building held nearly 37,000 square feet of work space, ten times more than the Menlo Park laboratory. During construction, Edison added four additional one-story buildings to house electrical, chemical, and metallurgical laboratories.

Edison secured approximately half of his 1,093 U.S. patents during the nearly 45 years he worked at West Orange, from 1887 to 1931. Initially, Edison continued working on electric lighting, but he quickly branched out into other fields. He developed his tinfoil phonograph into a commercial product and invented the first motion picture camera. During the 1890s, the laboratory designed and built the equipment used in Edison's ore milling project in northwestern New Jersey. Later, in the early twentieth century, Edison developed storage batteries and office dictating machines. He also organized companies to manufacture Portland cement and chemicals and designed a process to build molded cement houses.

In 1887, Edison wrote that "my ambition is to build up a great industrial works in the Orange Valley, starting in a small way and gradually working up." As the West Orange laboratory produced new inventions, Edison created new companies to manufacture and market them. By the 1920s, a large industrial complex employing thousands of workers surrounded the West Orange laboratory.

Edison with his laboratory staff on July 31, 1893. Edison hired experimenters, chemists, draftsmen, and machinists to help develop his inventions. The number of employees at West Orange fluctuated, depending on Edison's needs. In 1888, Edison employed 120 experimenters. A severe economic depression and the expense of Edison's ore milling project forced him to cut staff in the 1890s.

Edison displayed his mementos, honors, and awards in the library, the laboratory's most formal room. The *Genius of Electricity,* a large marble statue Edison purchased in Paris in 1889, stands in the center of the library. It represents the triumph of electric lighting over gas illumination.

The cubic foot of copper Edison received from the copper industry is displayed in the library. To show their appreciation for creating new markets for copper used in electric wires, copper producers asked Edison to name a gift. Mischievously, Edison asked for a solid cubic foot of copper, knowing that it would be difficult to cast a perfect cube. After eleven attempts, the copper producers gave Edison this cube on October 13, 1911.

Edison used the library to meet with his laboratory staff, company managers, and sales personnel. On July 20, 1914, Edison met with Edwin C. Barnes, a Chicago Ediphone dealer.

Edison managed the voluminous paperwork generated by his laboratory and companies at his library desk. In addition to business correspondence, Edison received many letters from the public, including requests from photograph and autograph seekers, charities, and amateur inventors soliciting technical advice.

Edison's library contains approximately 10,000 books, including bound sets of U.S. and foreign patents and technical publications in several languages. Edison and his employees consulted these books frequently during research projects.

Edison in his chemistry laboratory in 1904. Many of the inventions Edison and his staff devised in West Orange between 1887 and 1931, including phonograph records, storage batteries, and rubber, required extensive chemical research.

Edison experimenters L. Rosenstein, Ludwig Ott, Ignatius Goldstein, and Thomas Greenley are at work in the chemistry laboratory in 1910. Goldstein was an analytical chemist from Poland who devised methods to produce the nickel flake used in Edison's storage battery. Rosenstein was Goldstein's assistant, and Ludwig Ott was the son of Edison's machinist, John Ott.

Edison boasted that his laboratory machine shops could build anything from "a lady's watch to a locomotive." Workers in these shops cut and shaped the metal pieces used to make models of Edison's inventions. Machinists in the heavy machine shop made large equipment, including much of the machinery used in Edison's 1890s ore milling plant.

The precision machine shop, located on the laboratory's second floor directly above the heavy machine shop, contained smaller and more precise machine tools. Skilled machinists used these tools to fabricate small-scale prototypes.

Brothers Fred and John Ott test electric railroad equipment in the West Orange Laboratory courtyard. John Ott (left) was a skilled machinist who had worked for Edison since 1870. He supervised the West Orange precision machine shop. Fred Ott was also a machinist and worked in West Orange until Edison's death in 1931.

Edison expected to perform contract research for the electric utility industry. As a result, he dedicated an entire building to electrical experiments. Known as the Galvanometer Room, this building was constructed with copper nails and brass fittings because iron materials interfered with its sensitive magnetic testing equipment.

To increase the speed and efficiency of the invention process, Edison kept a well-equipped stock room at West Orange. The stock room contained a wide array of tools and supplies his workers might need during their research, including chemicals, metal stock, and such exotic material as ostrich feathers, porcupine quills, and seaweed.

The pattern shop made the wood patterns that were used to cast the metal parts of Edison's inventions. Although the laboratory had a blacksmith shop to forge metal and sharpen tools, patterns made in this shop were sent to local foundries for casting.

Shown here in January 1917, the photography studio and darkroom created images for advertising and publicity purposes. The studio also photographed Edison's inventions to document the research process or track design changes. Many of the photographs in this book were produced in this studio.

Edison punches his time card on February 11, 1921. Laboratory employees were required to record their work hours on time cards. Edison's managers used this information to generate payrolls and monitor expenses. Surviving time cards reveal that Edison typically worked between 50 and 60 hours a week.

Edison takes notes in the chemistry laboratory on December 15, 1928. Early in his career, Edison began keeping detailed research records. In the 1870s, he and his team kept notes on loose pages. When Edison began working on the electric light in 1878, he switched to bound notebooks, a practice he continued for the rest of his life. More than 5,000 laboratory notebooks survive in Edison's archive.

Edison often napped between long work sessions. In 1896 he told a reporter, "I can sleep anywhere, at any time, at a minute's notice." Although he could sleep on lab benches, his second wife, Mina, put a cot in the library so that he could nap undisturbed. Edison claimed that he needed little sleep. In the late 1920s he remarked, "Most men spend too large a portion of their lives in sleep—probably because they have no really absorbing work."

Edison eats lunch with six of his laboratory workers, nicknamed the "Insomnia Squad," on October 18, 1912.

Edison outside the office of his Ogdensburg, New Jersey, ore milling plant in 1895. During the 1890s, Edison developed technology to process low-grade iron ore. In 1889, he created the New Jersey & Pennsylvania Concentrating Works, which financed an experimental ore milling plant in northeastern New Jersey.

Edison's ore milling process used a series of large metal rolls to crush iron-bearing boulders into a fine powder. This powder was then dropped past powerful magnets, which separated out the iron. The iron was then formed into briquettes and shipped by railroad to foundries. The giant rolls shown in this photograph weighed 35 tons and could crush boulders weighing up to 5 tons.

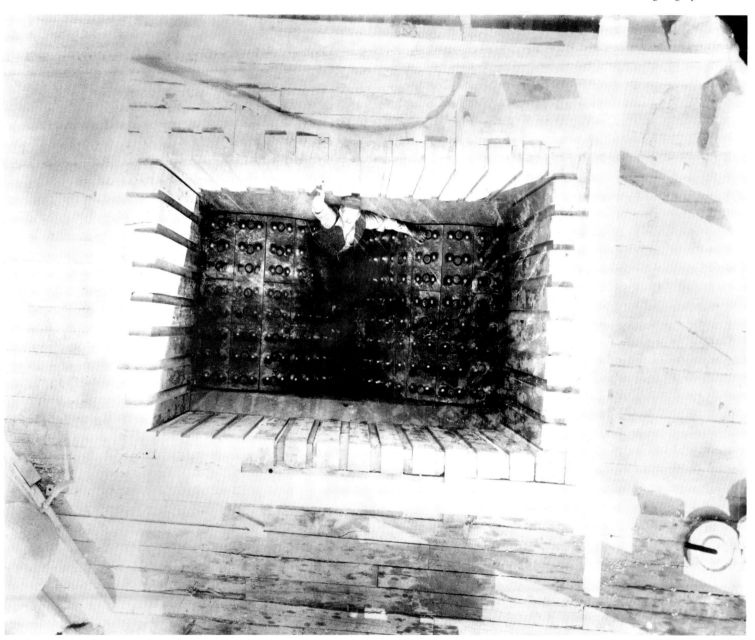

An Edison engineer in 1895 with the Corliss steam engine used to power the ore milling plant.

60

Employees of the New Jersey & Pennsylvania Concentrating Works at the Ogdensburg ore milling plant in 1893. Throughout the 1890s, operations at the ore milling plant were plagued by technical problems. By the late 1890s, Edison and his staff had resolved all of these problems, but the discovery of high-grade, low-cost iron ore in Minnesota's Mesabi Range made Edison's process impractical.

Edison became interested in X-rays in early 1896, following their discovery by the German scientist Wilhelm Roentgen. He improved the vacuum tubes used to generate X-rays and designed an apparatus to convert the invisible rays into visible light. By March 1896 he had invented the fluoroscope, a screen coated with calcium tungstate that produced X-ray images.

Charles Dally with X-ray apparatus, around May 1904. Edison abandoned X-ray research after Dally suffered severe radiation burns and subsequently died from cancer.

In 1899, Edison began developing an alkaline storage battery for electric vehicles. Existing lead-acid batteries were too heavy and unreliable for automobiles. Edison sought a lighter and more efficient battery and in 1903 introduced his Type E nickel-iron battery. Edison sold nearly 14,000 Type E batteries before technical problems forced him to recall them in 1904.

Edison (third from right) with prospectors searches for nickel in Sudbury, Ontario, in 1901. Edison needed nickel and cobalt for his storage battery. The August 1901 trip to Ontario persuaded him that the Sudbury district held promising supplies. Edison sent surveying teams to Sudbury between 1901 and 1904, and in 1905 he purchased the Darby Mine, near the town of Cobalt, only to abandon the mine in 1907, after replacing cobalt with less expensive minerals.

Edison and Colonel E. M. Bailey in a Bailey electric car, in 1910. In September of that year, two vehicles equipped with Edison storage batteries, a Bailey electric and a Detroit electric, completed a 1,000-mile endurance test through New England. The trip ended with an attempted ascent of Mount Washington in New Hampshire. High winds and rain prevented the cars from completing the eight-mile trip to the summit.

In 1909, after five years of research, Edison replaced the Type E storage battery with an improved version, the Type A. This photograph shows the complete line of Type A batteries in 1915.

A fleet of Standard Oil Company delivery trucks equipped with Edison storage batteries pulls up for a photograph in April 1912. Edison believed that storage battery–powered trucks would be more economical than gasoline vehicles. In 1910 he wrote, "The gasoline truck can never solve the trucking problem; three tons of coal turned into electricity and put into an electric truck and costing nine dollars will give more power than a ton of gasoline costing thirty two dollars."

Standard Plate Ice Company delivery truck in the West Orange laboratory courtyard in March 1915. By 1914, Edison storage batteries powered half the electric delivery vehicles used in the United States.

These Ward Baking Company delivery trucks are rolling in May 1915, equipped with the slogan "Modern Ideas in Baking" and Edison storage batteries.

Workers assemble Edison storage batteries in January 1915. Manufacturing was part of innovation at West Orange. Edison devised inventions in his laboratory, and then manufactured them in nearby factories. The laboratory also designed and made many of the machine tools used to manufacture Edison products. Edison controlled the manufacturing process to ensure quality and lower costs.

In 1899, Edison adapted his ore milling technology to the production of Portland cement. He organized the Edison Portland Cement Company and built a large manufacturing plant at New Village, near Stewartsville, New Jersey. By 1905 this plant produced 3,000 barrels of Portland cement a day.

Aerial view of the Edison Portland cement plant, New Village, New Jersey. Edison applied his knowledge of grinding iron ore to making cement, which required the crushing of limestone and cement rock into a fine grain. This mixture was then roasted in kilns—also designed by Edison, to increase production capacity and fuel efficiency.

In 1907, Edison began devising a process for constructing molded cement houses. In part, this was an effort to sell more Portland cement, but Edison also expected to lower housing costs. He claimed, "I believe [these houses] can be built by machinery in lots of 100 or more at one location for a price which will be so low that [they] can be purchased . . . by families whose total income is not more than $550 per annum."

Iron molds used to cast Edison cement houses, on the grounds of the West Orange laboratory in 1911. Edison claimed that these molds would allow a contractor to cast a house in six hours. Edison used this process to build a two-story garage on the grounds of Glenmont, but he never intended to enter the construction business. Instead, he allowed developers to use his technology royalty-free.

Developer Charles H. Ingersoll built these cement houses in Union, New Jersey, in 1919. Cement houses were also constructed in other New Jersey towns, including Montclair, Phillipsburg, and South Orange.

The White Construction Company used Edison Portland cement to build Yankee Stadium between 1921 and 1923. The stadium cost $2.5 million to construct and could seat 58,000 people. On opening day, April 18, 1923, the Yankees beat the Boston Red Sox, 4-1.

Edison and Harvey Firestone examine a specimen of rubber in his Fort Myers, Florida, laboratory on March 15, 1931. During the 1920s, the U.S. consumed about 70 percent of the world's rubber output, which was controlled by the British and Dutch. To prevent supply disruptions in the event of war, Henry Ford and Firestone encouraged Edison to find alternative domestic sources. In 1927, they created the Edison Botanic Research Corporation to support Edison's research.

By the 1920s, the West Orange laboratory was surrounded by a sprawling manufacturing complex that employed thousands of workers and produced phonographs, records, storage batteries, and other Edison inventions. Edison had fulfilled his 1887 goal: "My ambition is to build up a great Industrial Works in the Orange Valley starting in a small way & gradually working up."

# The Phonograph and Motion Pictures

## (1886–1930)

The West Orange laboratory devoted considerable attention to developing sound recording and motion picture technology. Edison returned to the phonograph in the fall of 1886, several months before he constructed the new laboratory. During the late 1880s, Edison designed the phonograph for use as an office dictating machine, but the unexpected popularity of coin-operated amusement phonographs in the early 1890s encouraged him to shift the focus of sound recordings from business to entertainment. In the late 1890s, Edison began manufacturing less expensive, simpler phonographs for home entertainment and a catalog of pre-recorded music on wax cylinders. In 1906, he re-introduced an office dictating machine, the Edison Business Phonograph.

Edison dominated the phonograph business in the early 1900s, but competition arose from the Victor Talking Machine Company, which sold a machine called the gramophone. Victor's disc records played longer musical selections and featured celebrity artists, including the Italian opera star Enrico Caruso. Edison responded by developing his own disc record, but he never regained his industry dominance. Competition from radio in the 1920s further threatened his phonograph business. By the late 1920s he controlled only 2 percent of the domestic record market. The Edison Company stopped manufacturing entertainment phonographs and records in 1929.

Edison announced his plan to invent "an instrument which does for the eye what the phonograph does for the ear, which is the recording and reproducing of things in motion" in October 1888. In the early 1890s, the West Orange laboratory had produced the kinetograph, the first motion picture camera, and the kinetoscope, which exhibited movies through a peephole. Edison's staff also built the first experimental motion picture studio, the Black Maria, where they filmed jugglers, exotic dancers, and other short action scenes.

As the motion picture business expanded in the late 1890s, inventors introduced screen film projectors and film makers began producing longer, more elaborate movies. Edison became a leading producer of motion picture equipment and films. He devoted little personal attention to his movie business, but he experimented on color and talking motion pictures. Rising production costs, increased competition, and the loss of his European market during World War I forced Edison to sell the business in 1918.

Edison with his improved phonograph in June 1888. Edison abandoned the tinfoil phonograph in the fall of 1878 as he shifted the focus of his research to the electric light. Edison returned to the phonograph in 1886, shortly before he began construction of the West Orange laboratory. The development of an improved cylinder phonograph became a leading research project at West Orange.

In the late 1880s, Edison redesigned the phonograph as an office dictating machine. The improved phonograph, which was powered by a chemical battery and electric motor instead of a hand crank, was equipped with start-stop controls, a new recorder-reproducer mechanism, and a removable wax cylinder. The improved phonograph enabled office workers to dictate letters onto wax cylinders. These recordings could then be mailed to correspondents or transcribed later by a stenographer.

In 1887, Edison began devising a talking doll. He designed a miniature phonograph and cylinder to place inside the doll's torso. The Edison Phonograph Works produced the phonograph mechanism and purchased the doll bodies from German toy manufacturers.

Edison Phonograph Works employees assemble talking dolls at West Orange in 1890. Despite Edison's plan to introduce the talking doll in time for the 1889 Christmas season, production problems delayed its release until January 1890. Edison manufactured 3,000 dolls in 1890, but consumer complaints about the fragile phonograph mechanism, which frequently malfunctioned, forced him to take the dolls off the market.

In 1889, Louis Glass, the general manager of the Pacific Phonograph Company, invented an attachment that turned the phonograph into a coin-operated machine. On November 23, 1889, Glass installed the first coin-operated phonograph in San Francisco's Palais Royal Saloon. For the price of a coin, patrons could hear a short song or comedy skit. The coin-operated machines changed the focus of the phonograph industry from business to entertainment.

Edison Phonograph Works employees manufacture coin-operated phonographs in 1890.

During the early 1890s, coin-operated phonographs were placed in railroad stations, saloons, hotels, and other public places throughout the United States. These machines were very profitable. From September 1889 to May 1890, the Pacific Phonograph Company earned more than $1,000 from the first machine it installed in the Palais Royal Saloon.

A group of girls in Salina, Kansas, listen to music on an Edison cylinder phonograph in the mid-1890s. Before the introduction of speaker horns in the late 1890s, listeners used rubber tubes equipped with earpieces.

ALL OF THESE MODELS WILL PLAY THE NEW BLUE AMBEROL RECORDS JUST AS WELL AS OUR AMBEROLA MODELS. SEE THE OTHER SIDE OF THIS PAGE FOR PARTICULARS

By 1900 Edison produced a line of affordable phonographs designed for home entertainment. Unlike earlier phonographs, these spring-driven machines did not have complicated recording features and they could only play pre-recorded music cylinders. Edison introduced the first of these less expensive machines, the Home phonograph, in 1896.

Edison relied on a national network of dealers, including J. K. O'Dea in Paterson, New Jersey, to sell his phonographs and records.

To increase sales, Edison experimented with solicitation, deploying door-to-door canvassers in 1909. These canvassers left a phonograph and some records in a potential customer's home for a free trial, and then returned in a few days to complete the sale. Edison believed that people would choose his phonograph over those of his competitors once they heard the quality of his recordings.

The West Orange laboratory included an experimental recording studio, or Music Room, where researchers devised the recording techniques used to mass produce musical records. Before the development of microphones in the 1920s, experimenters used horns to amplify and direct sound onto cylinder records.

Edison listens to recording artist Helen Davis accompanied by pianist Victor Young in the laboratory Music Room in 1912.
Edison was hearing impaired, but he personally evaluated and approved the artists and music recorded by his company.

Dutch opera singer Jacques Urlus makes a recording at Edison's New York City recording studio at 79 Fifth Avenue on March 30, 1916. Italian conductor Cesare Sodero, who served as Edison's music director from 1913 to 1925, conducts the orchestra. Although Edison had a recording studio at West Orange, his company operated a studio in New York to attract Broadway musicians and vocalists.

Edison examines his Diamond Disc phonograph record in 1921. Edison believed that the cylinder format produced superior sound, but competition from the Victor Talking Machine Company's disc record forced him to begin developing his own disc in 1909. Early Edison cylinders played up to two minutes of music. Edison released a four-minute cylinder in 1908, but the Victor disc could play seven minutes of music.

Musicians and models display an oversized Edison phonograph at an Atlantic City, New Jersey, trade show in August 1925. Early Edison phonographs were encased in plain wood cabinets with little or no ornamentation. During World War I, Edison began manufacturing disc phonographs encased in attractive cabinets designed to resemble fine furniture.

In this advertising photograph from December 1913, Edison poses with an early tinfoil phonograph and his dictating machine. Edison introduced his Business Phonograph in 1906. The Edison Company renamed this instrument the Edison Dictating Machine in 1912. In 1918, the Edison Dictating Machine became the Ediphone.

Office workers prepare correspondence on Edison Business Phonographs and typewriters. Edison marketed his dictating machines to the growing number of office managers employed by large corporations in the early twentieth century. Using Edison dictating machines, as company advertising promised, would make office work more productive and cut the time spent on routine paperwork. One ad noted that "all this freedom from routine gives you the opportunity you need for 'breaking away' from your desk."

Edison views a demonstration of his dictating machine in the West Orange library on July 20, 1914. Despite numerous photographs of Edison with the business phonograph, his staff recalled that he seldom used them. Typically, Edison answered his correspondence by jotting short notes on incoming letters. His office staff would then type a formal response.

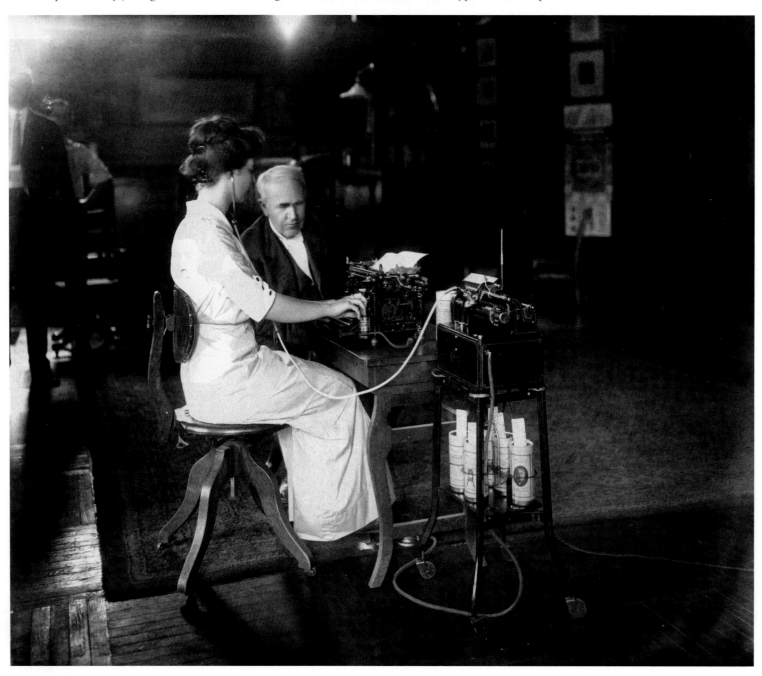

Edison dictating machines are displayed on a parade float in June 1915.

Edison company office workers transcribe correspondence dictated on Ediphones. By 1918
Edison's yearly Ediphone sales exceeded $1 million.

Edison exhibit at the Radio World's Fair, held at Madison Square Garden in New York City in September 1930. Despite its popularity in the 1920s, Edison believed that radio was a "fad" and resisted pressure to manufacture combination radio-phonographs until 1928.

Edison's first motion picture camera, the strip kinetograph, invented in West Orange in 1889. Edison's first motion picture apparatus used strips of photographs attached to a cylinder. Edison's staff designed the kinetograph after Edison replaced the paper-based photographs with images produced on rolls of celluloid photographic film.

Early Edison motion pictures were exhibited through the "peephole" kinetoscope. The Holland Brothers arcade on Broadway in New York City gave the first commercial demonstration of Edison's kinetoscope on April 14, 1894. By autumn of that year, kinetoscope parlors had opened in cities throughout the United States and Europe, including San Francisco, Atlantic City, and London.

Edison built this experimental motion picture studio in West Orange in February 1892. Nicknamed the "Black Maria" because it resembled police paddy wagons, it had an angled roof that could be raised to expose the interior stage to sunlight. The studio rested on a pivot and wooden track that allowed workers to turn it to follow the sun. Early Edison kinetoscope films featured short action scenes, including boxing matches, jugglers, and exotic dancers.

In January 1894, Edison experimenter William K. L. Dickson produced a series of short promotional films, including "The Record of a Sneeze." In this five-second motion picture, Edison employee Fred Ott takes a pinch of snuff and sneezes. The film, recorded in the Black Maria, was the first copyrighted motion picture in the United States.

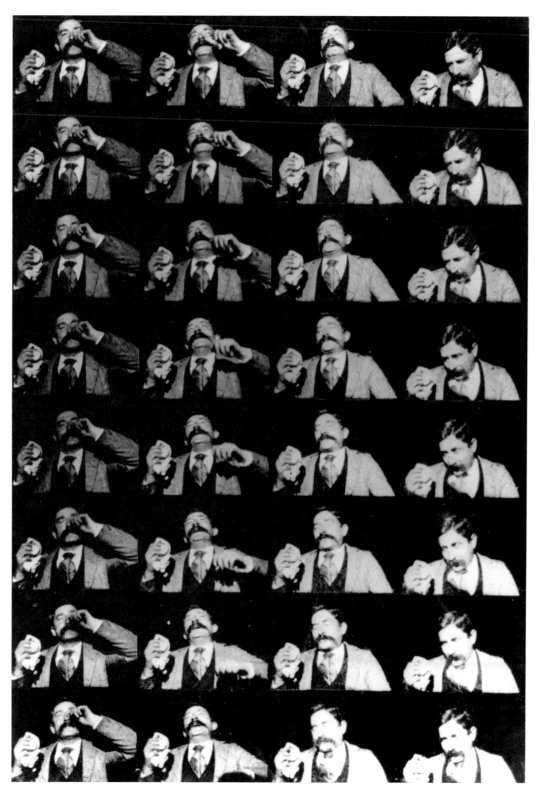

Audiences began to lose interest in the kinetoscope by the mid-1890s. To revive the film business, in 1896 Edison purchased the rights to a projector invented by C. Francis Jenkins and Thomas Armat and sold it under the name "Edison's Vitascope." Koster and Bial's Music Hall in New York City introduced the Vitascope to the public on April 23, 1896. In November 1897, Edison unveiled his own projector, the projectoscope.

Charles H. Kayser works on the motion picture camera in the West Orange laboratory around 1897. Kayser was an Edison experimenter who helped develop the motion picture camera in the late 1880s and early 1890s.

A scene from Edwin S. Porter's *Great Train Robbery,* released by Edison in 1903. Most films produced in the late 1890s were travelogues depicting unusual events or exotic locations. By 1900, movie audiences expected longer, more elaborate films with plots, narratives, and characters. *The Great Train Robbery* was one of Edison's most popular motion pictures.

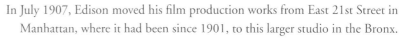

In July 1907, Edison moved his film production works from East 21st Street in Manhattan, where it had been since 1901, to this larger studio in the Bronx.

The interior of Edison's Bronx motion picture studio. The Bronx studio was large enough to permit the production of several films at the same time.

Edison with the licensees of the Motion Picture Patents Company in December 1908. Edison and eight other film producers created this company on December 18, 1908, to end costly patent litigation in the motion picture industry. The Motion Picture Patents Co. aggressively prosecuted unlicensed use of its motion picture technology and attempted to create a film distribution monopoly. In October 1915, the U.S. government won an antitrust suit against the company and it was dissolved.

Edison motion picture director J. Searle Dawley directs a scene from *Christian and Moor,* a costume drama filmed in Havana, Cuba, in August 1911. *Christian and Moor* was a love story about a Moorish princess and a Christian knight sent to negotiate a peace treaty with her father. Dawley directed many Edison films, including *Frankenstein* in 1910, the first film adaptation of Mary Shelley's novel.

James Oppenheim directs a scene from *Hope—A Red Cross Seal Story* at the Bronx studio in 1912. Produced in cooperation with the National Association for the Prevention of Tuberculosis, the film promoted the sale of Christmas seals to fight the disease. Its main character is John Harvey, a small-town banker and Christmas seal opponent whose fiancée contracts tuberculosis.

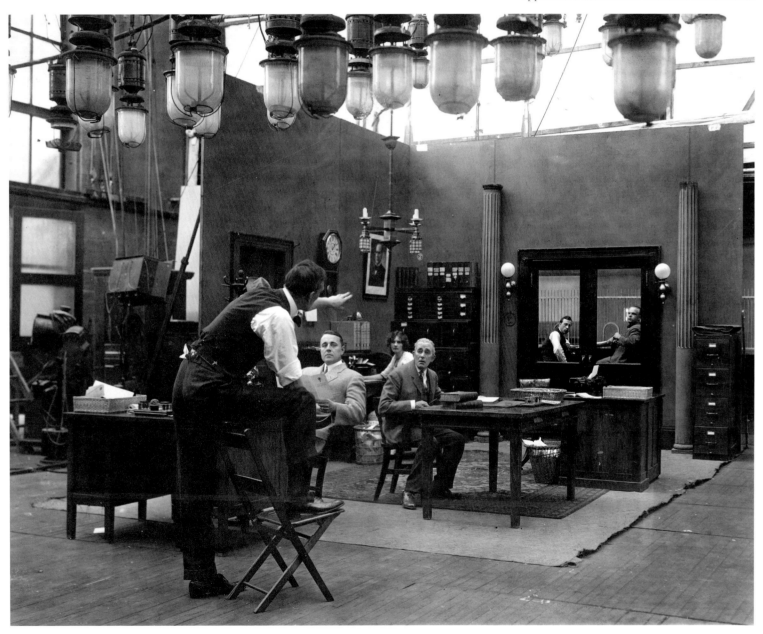

In 1910, Edison began devising a motion picture projector for use in homes and schools. Edison introduced the Home Projecting Kinetoscope in 1912. He also produced a library of educational films on various scientific topics for the machine. Neither the Home Projecting Kinetoscope nor the educational films were commercially successful.

A family watches a film on the Home Projecting Kinetoscope in this 1912 advertising photograph made at the Bronx studio.

Edison and George Eastman examine a motion picture camera in 1928 at Eastman's Rochester, New York, home. In 1889, Eastman provided the West Orange laboratory with the celluloid roll film used in Edison's early motion picture experiments. Eastman's film stock was 70 millimeters wide. To fit his motion picture apparatus, Edison split the stock in half, thus establishing the standard 35-millimeter film format.

# EDISON IN WORLD WAR I

## (1914–1918)

During World War I, Edison became a vocal supporter of military preparedness, a technical advisor to the U.S. Navy, and a military contractor. Edison recognized that new technologies were rapidly changing warfare. As he told the *New York Times* in November 1915, "Science is going to make war a terrible thing—too terrible to contemplate." He was not optimistic about the prospects for peace; consequently he believed the nation needed to be better prepared for war. In May 1915, he called for increased production of military supplies and the creation of government research laboratories to develop military technology.

Edison's views caught the attention of Navy Secretary Josephus Daniels. In July 1915, Daniels asked Edison to lead an advisory board to evaluate technical ideas for the navy. Staffed by representatives from eleven technical and scientific organizations, the Naval Consulting Board reviewed 110,000 inventions for the navy.

In 1917, Edison conducted research for the U.S. Navy. Much of this research focused on protecting military and commercial vessels from German submarine attacks. In the summer of 1917, he chartered a yacht to test methods for detecting submarines by sight, sound, and magnetic field. He also studied ship camouflage problems and recommended that vessels burn anthracite coal to reduce smoke emissions. Edison spent several weeks in Washington, D.C., in the fall of 1917 collecting data on Allied shipping losses. Learning that ships were using old routes and traveling through danger zones during daylight, he recommended that ships alter and vary their routes to avoid German submarines.

The war also affected Edison's business interests. Edison produced a special phonograph for military field use. He attempted, with little success, to sell his storage battery to the U.S. Navy's submarine fleet. The navy, however, awarded Edison a contract to supply batteries for battleship guns.

Edison became a chemical manufacturer during the war. He had been heavily dependent on German chemicals, particularly phenol, which was used to make phonograph records. Cut off from his European suppliers, Edison devised a process to make synthetic phenol and constructed chemical plants in Pennsylvania and Alabama to produce phenol, benzene, aniline dye, and other coal-based chemicals. Edison manufactured enough chemicals to supply his own needs and sell a surplus to other companies and the military.

On the evening of December 9, 1914, a fire swept through Edison's West Orange factory complex. The fire broke out at 5:30 P.M. in a motion picture film storage shed and spread quickly to the buildings used to produce phonographs and records. The laboratory was spared but thirteen factory buildings were destroyed before the fire was contained the following day.

Charles Edison, Edison, Carl H. Wilson, general manager of Thomas A. Edison, Incorporated, and an unidentified man survey the damage after the December 1914 fire. Building 24, where phonograph records were manufactured, stands in the background.

Edison promised his phonograph dealers and customers that he would quickly rebuild his manufacturing plant. In this January 16, 1915, photograph, Edison tracks reconstruction progress. By the end of December 1914, Edison had resumed cylinder record production. Disc record manufacturing restarted a month later.

In July 1915, Navy Secretary Josephus Daniels asked Edison to serve as president of the Naval Consulting Board, a civilian agency created to evaluate inventions submitted to the navy. Staffed by representatives from eleven technical organizations, the board reviewed more than 110,000 proposals. Edison, Daniels, and Assistant Navy Secretary Franklin D. Roosevelt pose with the board on October 7, 1915, on the steps of the State War and Navy Building in Washington, D.C.

Edison marched with the Naval Consulting Board in a New York City Preparedness Parade on June 16, 1916. The Preparedness Movement was a campaign by government agencies and private groups to promote military mobilization. Two days after this parade, Congress passed the National Defense Act of 1916, which increased the size of the military and created a federal National Guard.

Edison, with Navy Secretary Josephus Daniels, Miller Reese Hutchison, and his sons, Charles and Theodore, arrives at the Brooklyn Navy Yard for an inspection tour on October 12, 1914. During the war, Edison conducted research for the navy aimed at protecting Allied ships from enemy submarine attacks. After studying data on Allied shipping losses, he discovered that merchant ships were using well-known routes. He recommended that vessels vary shipping schedules and routes to avoid German submarines.

Robert Bachman, general manager of the Edison Storage Battery Company, Edison, and Miller Reese Hutchison, Edison's chief engineer, inspect submarine storage batteries on August 21, 1914. Edison hoped to sell storage batteries to the navy's submarine fleet. Submarines used lead-acid storage batteries for underwater propulsion. Lead-acid batteries, however, leaked sulfuric acid, which created dangerous chlorine gas when mixed with seawater. Edison believed that his nickel-iron batteries would be safer.

Edison on board the E-2 submarine at the Brooklyn Navy Yard in December 1915. The navy agreed to test Edison's battery on its E-2. The batteries were installed in November 1915, but early tests revealed that the batteries released dangerous hydrogen gas during recharging. On January 15, 1916, while the navy installed a new ventilation system on the E-2, Edison's batteries exploded, killing five workers and injuring ten.

Charles Edison and William H. Meadowcroft with the Laboratory Home Guards, one of several battalions Thomas A. Edison, Incorporated, organized to provide military drill instruction. A number of workers served in the military during the war, including Edison Storage Battery Company employee Chester W. Tuck, who belonged to the first artillery battery to engage the Germans in France.

Edison company employees assemble on Lakeside Avenue for the Fourth Liberty Loan Drive in September 1918. The federal government organized a series of bond sales called Liberty Loans to finance the war effort. Individuals with modest incomes, including farmers, teachers, and factory workers, purchased almost a third of the bonds sold during World War I by the Treasury Department.

Charles Edison addresses Edison company employees during the Fourth
Liberty Loan Drive in September 1918.

Soldiers load Army and Navy Diamond Disc Phonographs at the West Orange laboratory. To entertain soldiers and sailors in the field, Edison designed a special phonograph for military use. The Army and Navy model came in a sturdy wood box, weighed 100 pounds, and sold for $50. Edison sold these phonographs to the U.S. government or charitable organizations that donated them to military units.

Edison's first wife, Mary Stilwell, was born in Newark, New Jersey, on September 6, 1855. Mary was an employee of Edison's News Reporting Telegraph Company, which provided commercial information to local businesses. After a brief courtship, they were married on December 25, 1871.

# Family and Friends

## (1871–1931)

Edison married his first wife, Mary Stilwell, an employee of his News Reporting Telegraph Company, on December 25, 1871. They had three children: Marion, Thomas, Jr., and William Leslie. Edison provided Mary with a comfortable life, but there is evidence of tension in their marriage. In February 1872, Edison jotted in his notebook, "Mrs. Mary Edison My Wife Dearly Beloved Cannot invent Worth a Damn." This note may have reflected her lack of interest in Edison's work. Mary, for her part, was frustrated by Edison's long absences from home.

Mary died on August 9, 1884. The following year Edison met Mina Miller, the daughter of prominent Ohio business leader Lewis Miller. They were married on February 24, 1886, and moved into Glenmont, a thirteen-acre estate in Llewellyn Park, a planned residential community in West Orange, New Jersey. Thomas and Mina had three children: Madeleine, Charles, and Theodore. With more education than Mary, Mina was better prepared to be the wife of a famous inventor. Like Mary, Mina struggled with Edison's long work hours, but she skillfully managed a large and busy household.

Edison had many acquaintances, but Henry Ford became his closest friend during the last two decades of his life. They first met at an electric utility convention in 1896, when Edison encouraged Ford's idea to develop a gasoline-powered automobile. Edison barely remembered the encounter, but Ford became a lifelong admirer. Their friendship began in 1912, after Ford asked Edison to develop a generator, battery, and starting motor for his Model T.

Ford purchased the property next to Edison's Fort Myers winter home. The Edison and Ford families began to visit each other on a regular basis and frequently vacationed together. In 1914, Edison and Ford, accompanied by naturalist John Burroughs, traveled through the Florida Everglades, the first of several annual camping trips. Tire manufacturer Harvey Firestone joined them on their 1916 camping trip through the Adirondacks and Vermont's Green Mountains. Occasionally, they were joined by other dignitaries, including presidents Warren Harding and Calvin Coolidge.

In 1918, Edison contributed $5,000 to Ford's unsuccessful campaign for the U.S. Senate. Ford provided Edison with money to support his rubber research during the 1920s and, along with Harvey Firestone, became a principal stockholder of the Edison Botanic Research Corporation.

Thomas and Mary had three children. Their first child, Marion Estelle Edison, was born on February 18, 1873.

Thomas Alva Edison, Jr., Thomas and Mary's second child, was born on January 10, 1876. In a reference to Edison's telegraphy background, Marion and Thomas, Jr., were nicknamed "dot" and "dash."

William Leslie Edison, Thomas and Mary's third child, was born on October 26, 1878.

Marion Estelle Edison, around 1881. Marion became Edison's closest companion between her mother's death in 1884 and his remarriage in 1886. Marion attended the Bradford Academy in Bradford, Massachusetts. In the early 1890s, she moved to Europe and eventually married Oscar Oser, a German army officer. After World War I, Marion divorced Oser and returned to the U.S. She lived in Norwalk, Connecticut, until her death in 1956.

William Leslie (left) and Thomas Alva
Edison, Jr. (right), around 1883.

Mary Stilwell Edison, around 1883. Edison's income provided Mary with a comfortable life, but their marriage was strained by his long work hours and lack of interest in her social life. After the Edisons moved to Menlo Park, Mary felt increasingly isolated from her family and friends in Newark. She died unexpectedly on August 9, 1884.

Thomas A. Edison, Jr., in 1897. Tom Jr. attempted, without much success, to become an inventor like his father. After attending St. Paul's School in Concord, New Hampshire, he opened a small laboratory in Burlington, New Jersey. Tom Jr. invented an automobile spark timer and carburetor attachment, but he was unable to market these inventions. During the 1920s, he worked in his father's West Orange laboratory. Tom Jr. died on August 25, 1935.

William Leslie Edison, like his brother and father, also aspired to be an inventor. He served in the army during the Spanish-American War and World War I. In 1900, he graduated from Yale's Sheffield Scientific School. William managed an automobile garage in Washington, D.C., and invented a spark plug. In the 1920s he experimented with radio at a small lab in Wilmington, Delaware. He died on August 10, 1937.

Samuel Edison and his friend, James Symington, posed for this portrait in England in 1886. Edison financed Samuel's trip to Europe. Symington wrote Thomas from Liverpool on January 20, "We have seen the noblest of all the cathedrals of Europe and we have seen the pomp the chivalry and the life of the Middle Ages pass before us till we are cobwebbed and mouldy with the dust of antiquity."

Edison met his second wife, Mina Miller (1865–1947), while attending the World Industrial and Cotton Centennial Exposition in February 1885. By the following June, when he saw Mina again at a friend's summer cottage north of Boston, Edison was in love. He wrote in his diary, "Saw a lady who looked like Mina—got thinking about Mina and came near being run over by a street car."

Mina was the seventh child of Lewis and Mary Valinda Miller. Lewis Miller was an Akron, Ohio, inventor and manufacturer of agricultural machinery. In 1874, he co-founded (with John Heyl Vincent) the Chautauqua Institution, an educational and recreational retreat for Methodist Sunday school teachers in Western New York. In this 1885 photograph, Mina (top row right) poses with her parents and nine siblings at their Akron home, Oak Lawn.

Mina Miller (far left) with family and friends on the lawn of her
Akron, Ohio, home, Oak Lawn, around 1884.

In August 1885, Edison, accompanied by Marion and a few associates, visited the Miller family at Chautauqua. During this visit, Edison persuaded Mina to travel with his group through upstate New York and New Hampshire. Edison had taught Mina Morse code, enabling them to conduct their courtship in privacy. While riding through the White Mountains, Edison tapped out a marriage proposal on Mina's hand.

Family lore holds that Edison gave Mina a choice of living either in New York City or a more rural setting. Mina chose a house in the country. As a wedding present to Mina, Edison purchased Glenmont, a thirteen-acre estate, on January 20, 1886. Located in West Orange's Llewellyn Park, the first planned residential community in the United States, the property included a 29-room Queen Anne–style house, a greenhouse, and a barn.

Edison on the Glenmont lawn on June 30, 1917. Henry C. Pedder, an executive with a New York City dry goods merchant, built Glenmont between 1880 and 1882. Pedder lost the property in 1884 after he was caught embezzling from his employer. Edison purchased the estate for $125,000. Glenmont was the center of Edison family life until Mina's death in 1947. It is now part of Edison National Historic Site.

Madeleine Edison, Thomas and Mina's first child, was born on May 31, 1888.

Edison with Charles
and Madeleine Edison
at Glenmont. Charles,
Thomas and Mina's
second child, was born
on August 3, 1890.

Theodore Edison, Thomas and Mina's youngest child, as a baby. Theodore, born on July 10, 1898, was named after Mina's youngest brother, who died in the Spanish-American War.

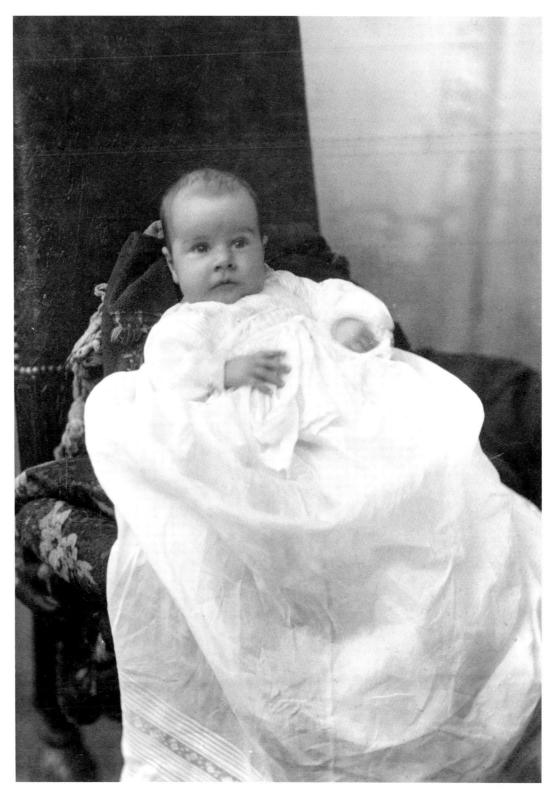

Mina with Charles and Madeleine Edison at Glenmont, around 1900.

Theodore Edison receives piano lessons from Lucy Bogue in the Glenmont den in 1907. Although Bogue was a servant, she became close to the Edison family. She served as Mina's secretary and companion, often traveled with the Edisons, and continued living at Glenmont after Mina's death in 1947.

Edison working at his desk in Glenmont's second-floor living room. The Edison family used this room for informal activities. Edison particularly enjoyed playing board games here with his children. Each evening, after dinner, Edison prepared notes for his next day's experiments. Madeleine recalled, "On Sundays this room would be strewn with newspapers. Father subscribed to about five papers and he read everything."

Theodore and Mina Edison,
around 1905.

Mina and Thomas Edison,
around 1908.

Edison in front of his Fort Myers, Florida, winter home, Seminole Lodge, in 1912. Edison purchased the property in Fort Myers during a March 1885 trip to Florida. Mina and Thomas honeymooned in Fort Myers in 1886. The Edison family typically spent part of each winter in Fort Myers.

Edison fishing with eleven-year-old Charles in Fort Myers in 1900. Edison did not participate in many leisure activities, but he enjoyed fishing during his Florida vacations.

Thomas, Mina, and Theodore Edison on the porch of Seminole Lodge, Fort Myers, Florida, 1909.

Edison and his family visit Emil Rathenau, a German electrical manufacturer, in Berlin during a 1911 vacation in Europe. During this trip the Edisons also visited England, France, and Switzerland.

Mina and Thomas Edison, with their three children, Charles, Madeleine, and Theodore, attend the 1911 Edison Field Day, an annual athletic competition for Edison company employees.

Madeleine Edison married aviator and inventor John Eyre Sloane at Glenmont on June 17, 1914. The first of their four sons, Thomas Edison Sloane, was born in 1916. Madeleine was interested in politics, and ran unsuccessfully for Congress in 1938. She died on February 14, 1979.

Charles Edison attended the Massachusetts Institute of Technology before he began working for his father's company in 1913. In 1926, he became president of Thomas A. Edison, Incorporated. During the 1930s, Charles held several positions in the Roosevelt Administration before becoming Navy Secretary in December 1939. In November 1940, he was elected governor of New Jersey, serving one three-year term. Charles retired from business in 1961 and died on July 31, 1969.

Thomas and Charles Edison, 1916.

Theodore Edison graduated from the Massachusetts Institute of Technology in 1923 with a physics degree. Theodore became an inventor, eventually securing 80 U.S. patents. During the 1920s, he worked on radio and electric sound recording at the West Orange laboratory. In the 1930s, he opened his own laboratory and created Calibron Industries, Incorporated, an engineering consulting firm. Later in life, he became an environmentalist and philanthropist. He died on November 24, 1992.

Henry Ford greets Edison at Glenmont on Edison's 80th birthday in 1927. From 1912 to 1931, Edison and Ford were close friends. When they met in 1896 at an electric utility convention, Edison supported Ford's gasoline-powered automobile ideas. Their friendship began in 1912, when Ford asked Edison to develop a generator, battery, and starting motor for his Model T.

Edison and Ford frequently traveled together. In the fall of 1915, Thomas and Mina traveled with Henry and Clara Ford to the Panama Pacific Exhibition in San Francisco. During this trip they visited botanist Luther Burbank, photographed here with Edison, Ford, and a large crowd of admirers in Santa Rosa, California.

Edison, Harvey Firestone, Jr., R. J. H. DeLoach, John Burroughs, Henry Ford, and Harvey Firestone examine the old Evans Mill near Bolan Springs, Virginia, on August 23, 1918. During their 1918 camping trip, Edison and his friends toured the Great Smoky Mountains. DeLoach was a friend of Burroughs and a college professor from Georgia.

President Warren G. Harding joined Edison, Ford, and Firestone for their 1921 camping trip through Maryland, Virginia, and West Virginia. In this photograph, Edison, Ford, and Harding read newspapers in their camp outside Hagerstown, Maryland, on July 24, 1921.

Thomas and Mina Edison cutting his birthday cake at Glenmont on his 80th birthday, February 11, 1927.

Thomas and Mina Edison at Fort Myers on his 84th birthday, February 11, 1931. After Edison's death, Mina married Edward E. Hughes, a childhood friend and retired steel executive, on October 30, 1935. Hughes died on January 20, 1940. Mina continued to live at Glenmont until her death on August 24, 1947.

# FAME AND LEGACY

Beyond the telegraph industry, Edison was not widely known before he introduced the phonograph in December 1877. The phonograph made Edison famous. In early 1878, visitors began flocking to Menlo Park to see the new invention. For the first time, Edison began receiving fan mail, including letters requesting his photograph or soliciting his advice. Newspaper reporters, who had nicknamed him the "Wizard of Menlo Park," eagerly sought interviews with Edison.

By cultivating good relations with newspaper reporters, Edison helped shape his public image, but he was ambivalent about his celebrity status. He appreciated the value of his fame for attracting potential investors and used his name, image, and reputation to market his inventions. Dealing with reporters and the steady stream of laboratory visitors and correspondence, however, distracted Edison from his work. Edison received many invitations to join organizations, to attend dinners or give public speeches, most of which he politely declined. Occasionally, he stumbled in published interviews, leading to unfavorable publicity. In an October 1910 interview, for example, he doubted the immortality of the human soul. His views generated critical editorials and bags of hate mail.

Edison received accolades throughout his career, but he seemed to tolerate the attention more in his declining years. In May 1925, the Edison Pioneers, an organization of early Edison employees, erected a commemorative tablet at Menlo Park. Edison received the Congressional Medal in 1928 and an honorary Academy Award in 1929. Henry Ford reconstructed the Menlo Park laboratory at his museum in Dearborn, Michigan. Its dedication in October 1929 was a highlight of Light's Golden Jubilee, the 50th anniversary of Edison's electric light. Perhaps the ultimate tribute came after Edison's funeral on October 21, 1931, when President Herbert Hoover asked the nation to dim its lights for one minute at 10:00 P.M.

Although Edison experienced some notable failures, he had a profound impact on the American economy. Shortly after his death in 1931, the *Wall Street Journal* estimated that the industries based on his inventions exceeded a value of $15 billion. Perhaps his greatest achievements were his Menlo Park and West Orange laboratories. These well-equipped laboratories, staffed by talented experimenters, were the forerunners of the modern industrial research facilities that continue to develop new technologies.

Late-nineteenth-century technical exhibitions were an important source of information about new inventions. At the 1889 Paris Universal Exposition, Edison mounted a large exhibit of his inventions, including his telephone transmitter, phonograph, and electric light. Edison's display occupied almost a third of the space allotted the United States in the exposition's Palace of Mechanical Industries.

Edison's Paris exhibit gave many Europeans their first glimpse of the phonograph and the electric light. The exhibit featured a large globe made out of 13,000 incandescent lamps. "In the center of this cluster of lamps," the St. Joseph, Missouri, *Gazette* reported in July 1889, "is a large hairpin-shaped carbon which flashes out a bright red colored light which produces a wonderfully brilliant effect and lights up the whole machinery hall."

This delegation, representing the Japanese Chamber of Commerce, visited Edison in October 1909 and is typical of the many guests he received at West Orange. According to Edison's official biographer, "A very large part of the visiting is done by scientific bodies and societies, and then the whole place will be turned over to hundreds of eager, well dressed men and women, anxious to see everything and to be photographed in the big courtyard around the central hero."

A group of West Orange schoolboys visit Edison in 1913.

Aviator Orville Wright (third from the left) visited Edison on December 17, 1913. Mina (far left), Madeleine (second from the left), and John Sloane, Madeleine's fiancé (second from right) joined Edison and Wright for this photograph.

Edison met Rudolf Diesel in the library on April 12, 1912. Diesel, a German engineer who invented the diesel engine in 1893, came to the United States with a delegation of German scientists and engineers studying American industrial museums.

Edison's secretary, William H. Meadowcroft, with John Philip Sousa and James Francis Cooke, editor of *Etude Magazine*, at the West Orange laboratory on May 16, 1923. Sousa was a popular composer and bandleader. In 1906, Sousa criticized recorded music, claiming that it would "reduce the expression of music to a mathematical system of megaphones, wheels, cogs, disks, cylinders and all manner of revolving things," but he was viewing the phonograph more favorably by the 1920s.

Newspaper reports of Edison's phonograph and electric lamp made him an international celebrity. Edison cultivated good relations with reporters, who created his image as a tireless inventor who could solve any technical problem. By the early 1880s, newspapers had dubbed Edison the "Wizard of Menlo Park," a persona he maintained for the rest of his life.

On June 15, 1915, Edison was awarded an honorary doctor of science degree from Princeton University. In this photograph, Edison walks with Princeton Graduate School dean Andrew F. West (middle) and Colonel George W. Goethals, recipient of an honorary doctor of laws degree. Goethals was an Army Corps of Engineers officer who supervised the construction of the Panama Canal from 1907 to 1914.

On May 16, 1925, the Edison Pioneers, an organization of early Edison employees, dedicated a commemorative tablet on the site of Edison's Menlo Park laboratory. Thomas and Mina Edison attended the unveiling ceremony, which featured speeches by New Jersey governor George S. Silzer and General Electric chairman Edwin W. Rice, Jr.

Edison and eight other industrialists were honored at a dinner on October 25, 1928, at the Astor Hotel in New York. The press noted that these leaders, who ran companies worth more than $10 million, had humble backgrounds. From left to right are Harvey Firestone; Sears, Roebuck & Company president Julius Rosenwald; Edison; tea merchant Thomas Lipton; Bethlehem Steel Company president Charles M. Schwab; Henry Ford; automaker Walter Chrysler; Eastman Kodak founder George Eastman; and Chicago meatpacker Thomas E. Wilson.

At a ceremony broadcast to thirty million radio listeners on October 28, 1928, Treasury secretary Andrew W. Mellon presented Edison with the Congressional Medal for "illuminating the path of progress through the development and application of inventions that have revolutionized civilization in the last century." Princeton University president John Grier and British embassy official Ronald Campbell also attended the ceremony. Campbell returned Edison's original phonograph, which had been on display at London's South Kensington Museum since 1880.

Edison with the judges of the 1929 Edison Scholarship Contest, July 29, 1929. From left to right are Lewis Perry, headmaster of Philips Exeter Academy; George Eastman; Charles Lindbergh; Edison; Henry Ford; and Samuel W. Stratton, president of the Massachusetts Institute of Technology. The contest evaluated candidates on the basis of scientific knowledge, character, and ambition. The 1929 winner, Wilbur B. Huston, received a $2,500 scholarship, which he used to attend the Massachusetts Institute of Technology.

Edison, Henry Ford, and former Edison assistant Francis Jehl re-enact the invention of the incandescent electric lamp on October 21, 1929. Throughout 1929, special events commemorated the 50th anniversary of the electric lamp, Light's Golden Jubilee, but the focus of the celebration was on the dedication of Henry Ford's Edison Institute of Technology and Greenfield Village. Greenfield Village, a collection of historic buildings, included Edison's reconstructed Menlo Park Laboratory and is open to the public today.

Thomas and Mina Edison arrived at Greenfield Village for the Light's Golden Jubilee on the morning of October 21, 1929. They were accompanied by President Herbert Hoover and Mrs. Hoover, and traveled from Detroit on a vintage 1860 train similar to the one used by the Grand Trunk Railroad during Edison's youth.

President Hoover and Henry Ford on the second floor of the reconstructed Menlo Park Laboratory with Edison and Francis Jehl as they examine a vacuum pump used in their original lamp experiments.

Lucius W. Hitchcock, a noted artist and book illustrator, painted Edison's last portrait from life at Glenmont on June 30, 1931. Hitchcock's Edison portrait now hangs in Glenmont's second-floor living room, the same room in which Edison posed for the portrait.

Suffering from diabetes and stomach ailments, Edison's health deteriorated considerably in his last year. He collapsed at Glenmont shortly after he was photographed leaving his doctor's office in Morristown, New Jersey, in July 1931. By September his kidneys began to fail, and he lapsed into a coma in early October. Edison died at the age of 84 on October 18, 1931.

Upon Edison's death the family closed the laboratory and factories for his funeral. For two days, October 19 and 20, 1931, an honor guard of selected Edison employees stood vigil over Edison's casket in the library as the public paid their respects. The family held a private funeral for Edison at Glenmont on October 21, 1931, followed by interment at Rosedale Cemetery in Orange, New Jersey.

On October 19 and 20, 1931, men, women, and children waited in long lines outside the West Orange laboratory to view Edison's body.

A crowd waits in the rain to see the May 16, 1940, world premiere of *Edison the Man* at the Hollywood Theater in East Orange, New Jersey. *Edison the Man,* which starred Spencer Tracy and depicted the invention of the phonograph and electric light at Menlo Park, was one of two Edison films released by Metro-Goldwyn-Mayer that year. *Young Tom Edison,* starring Mickey Rooney, premiered in Port Huron, Michigan, on February 11.

The premiere of *Edison the Man* was part of a three-day celebration called the "Pageant of Progress." The festivities included parades and a ball held at the Orange, New Jersey, armory, attended by Edison's widow, Mina Edison Hughes, Charles Edison, and 4,000 guests. Local merchants celebrated the premiere by decorating their windows with Edison photographs and memorabilia.

A West Orange store commemorates Edison's achievements during the "Pageant of Progress" in May 1940. Despite pouring rain during the premiere of *Edison the Man,* large crowds gathered to see the film's stars, Spencer Tracy and Rita Johnson. As one woman told a reporter, "My family for three generations has worked for Edison, and I'd be glad to wait two days to see the man who is playing his part in the movie."

Thomas A. Edison Incorporated continued to manufacture the Ediphone in the 1930s and 1940s. In 1951, the company gave the Ediphone a sleeker, more streamlined design, replaced its cumbersome cylinder with small, flexible discs, and renamed it the Edison Voicewriter.

To appeal to the growing number of business travelers in the 1950s, Thomas A. Edison Incorporated introduced the Voicewriter-Portable in 1952. This advertising photograph shows the machine's practicality for air travelers.

This bust of Edison, sculptured by Evelyn Beatrice Longman, stands on the grounds of the Naval Research Laboratory in Washington, D.C. Donated by the Thomas Alva Edison Foundation and unveiled on December 3, 1953, the bust commemorates Edison's role in creating the laboratory. As president of the Naval Consulting Board, Edison encouraged the Navy to open a laboratory to develop military technology. Congress allocated funds for the facility in 1918 and construction began in 1920.

# NOTES ON THE PHOTOGRAPHS

These notes, listed by page number, attempt to include all aspects known of the photographs. Each of the photographs is identified by the page number, photograph's title or description, photographer and collection, archive, and call or box number when applicable. Although every attempt was made to collect all available data, in some cases complete data was unavailable due to the age and condition of some of the photographs and records.

**134** MARION EDISON
Edison National Historic Site
14.312.3

**135** THOMAS EDISON, JR.
Edison National Historic Site
14.314.03

**136** WILLIAM EDISON
Edison National Historic Site
14.315.03

**137** MARION EDISON
Edison National Historic Site
14.312.5

**138** WILLIAM AND THOMAS
Edison National Historic Site
14.335.3

**139** MARY EDISON
Edison National Historic Site
14.350.6

**140** THOMAS EDISON, JR.
Edison National Historic Site
14.314.08

**141** WILLIAM EDISON
Edison National Historic Site
14.315.4

**142** SAMUEL EDISON
Edison National Historic Site
14.300.8

**143** MINA MILLER
Edison National Historic Site
14.351.12

**144** MILLER FAMILY
Edison National Historic Site
14.340.49

**145** MINA MILLER
Edison National Historic Site
14.340.50

**146** MILLER HOME
Edison National Historic Site
14.340.22

**147** GLENMONT
Edison National Historic Site
12.420.1

**148** EDISON AT GLENMONT
Edison National Historic Site
14.220.47

**149** MADELEINE EDISON
Edison National Historic Site
14.311.6

**150** CHARLES AND MADELEINE
EDISON
Edison National Historic Site
14.330.6

**151** THEODORE EDISON
Edison National Historic Site
14.313.2

**152** MINA AND CHARLES
Edison National Historic Site
14.354.2

**153** THEODORE EDISON
Edison National Historic Site
14.313.7

**154** EDISON AT WORK
Edison National Historic Site
14.220.83

**155** THEODORE AND MINA
Edison National Historic Site
14.354.9

**156** MINA AND THOMAS
Edison National Historic Site
14.355.15

**157** EDISON AT FORT MYERS
Edison National Historic Site
14.400.42

**158** THOMAS AND CHARLES
Edison National Historic Site
14.310.10

**159** MINA AND THEODORE
Edison National Historic Site
14.330.8

**160** EMIL RATHENAU
Edison National Historic Site
14.225.175

**161** MINA AND THOMAS
Edison National Historic Site
14.330.10

**162** MADELEINE'S MARRIAGE
Edison National Historic Site
14.311.17

**163** CHARLES EDISON
Edison National Historic Site
14.310.29

**164** THOMAS AND CHARLES
Edison National Historic Site
14.310.19

**165** THEODORE EDISON
Edison National Historic Site
14.313.9

**166** HENRY FORD
Edison National Historic Site
14.110.61

**167** LUTHER BURBANK
Edison National Historic Site
14.130.100

**168** EVANS MILL
Edison National Historic Site
14.225.93

**170** PRESIDENT HARDING
Edison National Historic Site
14.475.260

**171** EDISON'S BIRTHDAY
Edison National Historic Site
14.110.10

**172** THOMAS AND MINA
Edison National Historic Site
14.110.57

**174** UNIVERSAL EXPOSITION
Edison National Historic Site
18.100.28

**175** PARIS EXHIBIT
Edison National Historic Site
18.100.6

**176** JAPANESE CHAMBER OF
COMMERCE
Edison National Historic Site
14.820.16

**177** WEST ORANGE BOYS
Edison National Historic Site
14.820.31

**178** ORVILLE WRIGHT
Edison National Historic Site
14.820.28

**179** RUDOLPH DIESEL
Edison National Historic Site
14.225.130

**180** WEST ORANGE LAB
Edison National Historic Site
14.225.121

**181** WIZARD OF MENLO PARK
Edison National Historic Site
wizard

**182** EDISON'S GRADUATION
Edison National Historic Site
14.130.60

Edison talks to young people in 1915 at the Panama Pacific Exposition, San Francisco.